Catalogue of Ripening

Catalogue of Ripening

Sabrina Guo

Children's Art Foundation–Stone Soup Inc.
Santa Cruz, California

Book design by Joe Ewart
Typeset in Quincy and Neue Haas Unica

ISBN: 978-0-89409-142-1 (paperback)
ISBN: 978-0-89409-143-8 (e-book)

Library of Congress Control Number: 2022943726

www.stonesoup.com

Printed in the United States of America

First edition

Cover: *Sun Goddess* by Sage Millen, 13 (British Columbia, Canada)
This photograph originally appeared in the February 2022 issue of
Stone Soup.

To my parents, Spencer and Eva,
and my brother, Brian,
for always loving and supporting me.

TABLE OF CONTENTS

At first, it was just a name: Sabrina Guo. A student whose work
was repeatedly published in *Stone Soup*. In what was at the time
our roughly forty-five years of publishing, there were other
authors who were published multiple times. However, it soon
became evident that Sabrina was besting our records. Besides
repeated acceptances to the magazine, she was frequently
sweeping our contests, reviewing books for our blog, and
energetically corresponding with all of us via email.

Then, in the summer of 2018, Sabrina did something
remarkable. The previous winter, my colleagues and I had
decided that we would like to begin offering a space in *Stone
Soup* for work by refugee youth whose lives had been upended
by uncontrollable violence. But with limited resources, we
needed volunteers with vision to help us out. So, we sent an
appeal through our weekly newsletter.

A few months later, I got an email from twelve-year-
old Sabrina. In the intervening months, Sabrina had been
conducting research on photographers and artists working in
refugee camps. She had found a film director and storytelling
instructor working in a Syrian refugee camp—Laura Doggett,
founder of the Another Kind of Girl Collective—and reached
out to see if she could interview her via Skype and publish it
on the Stone Soup Blog.

Inspired by Laura's efforts, and in consultation with
Sabrina, we were finally able to launch the Stone Soup Refugee
Project. It now has its own web portal, and we have ongoing
programs in refugee camps in multiple countries. Sabrina
provided the spark we needed.

Shortly after this, I began to refer to Sabrina, fondly but
very earnestly, as a "force of nature." It had become clear to me
that if Sabrina wrote and asked someone at *Stone Soup* to do
something, then the most practical course of action was to do
that something—and now—as she was not going to let it drop.
From my earliest awareness of Sabrina, she has been a young
person with tremendous creative vision, poise, confidence,
determination, and a very clear sense of how to get things done.

This truly came to the forefront during the pandemic, when
she did something utterly extraordinary. She convinced her
parents to use her college fund to purchase protective gear
for hospitals and care homes in her region. With her savings

as seed money, she raised tens of thousands of dollars and did something that few of us ever do: she saved lives. Sabrina has additionally started several nonprofits, most of which are devoted to helping girls prosper in what remains an unequal world. I bring up all of this not only to highlight the fact that Sabrina is an extraordinary young woman, but because her identity as a young social activist is essential to understanding her collection of poetry.

From poems that ponder the fate of her family—past and future—in a world facing climate crisis after crisis to ones that document the earliest victims of the COVID-19 pandemic to a tribute to the journalist Marie Colvin, who was killed while covering the Syrian Civil War, Sabrina faces the biggest political issues of our time head on, with clear eyes and courage. In other, seemingly more personal poems, she espouses a worldview that places responsibility for social action on each of us, as individuals. For example, in the poem, "The Money Tree," a lovely work that brilliantly evokes one of her culturally Chinese family's holiday traditions, she concludes with this observation:

> and sometimes I lay
> a crooked leaf over
> a straight one
>
> in the hopes it might
> correct itself,
>
> because isn't luck
> something that's made?

This is the speculation of a person who is actively seeking to change the world. Nothing will change for the better if one does nothing, if one simply observes the pattern. Luck doesn't just happen. You make your luck. You make your life, as well as the world you live in.

At one point, I traveled to New York, in part, to meet Sabrina and her parents. What can I say? Such grace. Such presence. Such a welcoming manner. Sabrina, now sixteen, has built a CV that is longer and possesses more depth than most adults will ever achieve. From literary prizes to violin performances, to speaking engagements, television appearances, and organizations started and funded, Sabrina has become someone I personally admire. And despite her abilities as a poet and musician and her work in activism, she assures me she sleeps, has friends, a teenage social life, and is a reasonably normal high school student!

And so, it is with great pride that I am writing the foreword to *Catalogue of Ripening*, Sabrina Guo's debut poetry chapbook. *Stone Soup*'s age cutoff is fourteen. Sabrina is now sixteen. This is the first *Stone Soup*-published volume to reflect the artistic growth—the "ripening"—of a *Stone Soup* writer who has moved into the next phase of her writing life. There is a thematic depth and complexity to many of these poems that marks them as the works of a rapidly developing writer— an author whose mind is quickening as she begins to move deeper into the person she is becoming. As you read this volume, you will encounter a profound talent.

—William Rubel
Co-founder & executive director of Stone Soup-The Children's Art Foundation

There is no charm equal to tenderness of heart.
— Jane Austen

坏事好事 (HUÀI SHÌ HǍO SHÌ; EVIL THINGS, GOOD THINGS)

Every New Year's Eve,
my friend smashes six pomegranates
on her lawn, and when I ask why,
she says it is because
she is Greek. I want to understand what she means—

on the Internet, I find Persephone: abducted
by Hades, her mother Demeter drying
the Earth into a cold, long winter
until Zeus arranged
her daughter's return—

because she ate six pomegranate seeds,
she returns to Hades
to spend each winter in darkness. I wonder
if the more my friend's
pomegranate seeds spread,

the more luck and fertility
there will be in the new year—
not so different from
my own need to squeeze
the eyedropper six times,

never four, because my parents
say four is unlucky, since the word
for four in Chinese, Sì,
sounds almost identical to *death*, Sǐ,
the only difference, the level of inflection.
It seems strange that six

would have been so unlucky, but without them
there wouldn't be seasons to wish for.
And when she tells me about the pomegranate pulp,
tiny seeds clinging to frozen grass
in the January cold, I understand what she means.

AUBADE: ROSYLN

Bluebells
bring faith—
teardrops
waiting to be
unfurled, tendrils
on their stem
still waiting to grow,
eager for the beauty
that a bell withholds.
All other flowers blur
behind these
bells of wisdom.

Back in the old
house in Roslyn,
we had a mini garden
with orange tulips
gleaming
in the fading moonlight
in fertile brown soil,
earthy and sweet,
and I would fold
in my beads of fertilizer—
green pearls
were what I called them
as a child—

each pearl giving rise
to its most perfect plant:
beingness
folded inside,
all as one,
like a soul
in a body.

OPEN SUN

"I watched my baby girl die slowly."
—*CNN, July 10, 2019*

On TV, I watch the colorful dreams of children
shrivel in the open sun.

Held in cages, each family
loses hope that summer will end—the rusting
fences, the humanity of drinking rain.
Metal bowls scratching the wooden tables—

in a video, the ribs of malnourished babies protrude
from tattered clothes, from rows
of huddled families, aluminum foil blankets.

Down the road
from my house, I see
red sand beaches, gulls fighting
over small nests of fries, and I
cup the sand in my hands, hoping
summer won't end.

At the beach, my father brings buckets
of water to me, my mother,
the sandcastle molds—and still
the castle washes away on the shore.
In its place, a heap of mud.

On the news most nights, I watch
babies with puke-dried bibs
around their necks. I think of them
for days.

From his place in the sand, my father
shouts, *Be careful, be careful*—still I run
into the sea, laugh, keep running.

65 CYBELE

In the summer
when it pours,
a lake forms

in my backyard,
rivulets soaking
the grass—

a jungle monsoon
thousands
of miles away.

My boots heavy
in the rain,
I share my sorrow

with calming droplets
and hear my truth,
recall that

I was born in Queens,
of which I remember little
except for smoke unfurling

from apartment roofs
before my family moved
to Long Island,

which is hardly an island
at all. It's not tropical
for one thing, and you don't need

a boat or a plane
to get there. In Oyster Bay,
it snows in the winter,

cold enough for hot
cocoa and heavy coats.

The blades of my skates
cut into the ice
but they don't break the surface

as the frozen asteroid
65 Cybele did
four-point-five billion

years ago, breaking off
a chunk of rock
that then became the moon.

In concert with the sun,
that solar nebula,
collapsed by gravity,

spread its tendrils
over the Earth, melted
the ice that remained

into bodies of water.
Water is made of molecules
and molecules

are made of atoms
and atoms are made
of neutrons, electrons,

and protons—
opposite forces,
that need each other

to form life.
Everything a process—
an experience

of coming
into contact
with the other.

AUBADE WHILE DOING MY MAKEUP

Even my reflection can see
the violin in the corner of my bedroom
needs more polish and sanding.

The white dress, unworn, hangs
down the piano bench—lace unfurling.

I shift to center. She reads me.
The red choker tightens around her neck.

I look down. The carpet's dust
under my toenails, my feet anchored
as she binds my ankles
with weeds. I kick the carpet

as she laughs.
I fill in my eyebrows a shade too dark.

You timid girl, she says.
I cap the brow pencil.

She doesn't know that
I'll sit on that piano bench later
and tattoo my thigh, that I'll think
of her words as they vibrate through skin.

That, as my eyes roll back, I'll know
she's watching, beautiful and fried.

PINK MILK

I am seven, exploring
the koi fish under the cherry blossoms.

Begrudgingly, I drink milk
every night. Although
I am seven, I am shrinking.

The midnight breath of owls
as it brushes past my eyelashes.
A comic that comes
in the mail every day—
these are the only things
I look forward to.

Besides the burnt toast
my father and I devour
every morning, I love Mum's
orange jam.

The doctor says
I need more calcium—
my bones, weakening. I should
be growing.

Each day, I grow
with the koi. Silent, gentle—
those soft pink petals
scattering across the pond.

KYOTO

The moon
	like a chestnut

	waiting for a squirrel
to crack it,

brown dust
	of prosperity

	showering over
every couple.

The floating
	sweet and sour
scent of fried fish,

	stabbed
with wood picks.

Takoyaki
	flipped over a pan,

	fried milk,
rich and creamy inside,

a gold coating—

	the kind that makes
my throat itch.

	Fresh caramels
littering the ground,
	melting from the heat.

The moon
	peeling itself
with relief.

THE MONEY TREE

There is a money tree
in my living room

with a braided
fishtail trunk

and of these five
interwoven strands,

only one of them has
visible veins pumping water

to those plumed green leaves
like dollar bills.

For Chinese New Year,
we don't hang coin garlands

or paper cranes
for Liu Haichan,

the toad in the moon,
the God of Wealth—

no. My mother waters
the leaves,

and my cat likes
to eat them while my father

chases her away
for fear of bad luck;

me, I just notice
the tree bending over

and sometimes I lay
a crooked leaf over
a straight one

in the hopes it might
correct itself,

because isn't luck
something that's made?

SACRIFICE

*Dedicated to all those who died in the Marjorie Stoneman
Douglas High School shooting on Feb. 14, 2018*

In old Christian myths
women and children
were entombed—

as protection against
weather and war:
virgins lost

to German lakes,
infants buried under
fortresses and bridges.

But the songs
of the sacrificed
are never silent—

their wailing is
wind over the ocean.

The moment Peter Wang
heard the blasts
of the AR-15 semiautomatic,

the screams,
he held the door open
for his classmates

and teachers, bound
by his Junior Reserve uniform
to act with honor.

Gold-pinned,
black insignia stitched
into the shape of wings

across his shoulders—
a hero, even as fear
crowded his veins.

Newsprint can't capture
Peter Wang's casket
as it is carried away,

under stars and stripes.
He was buried
with a Medal of Heroism,

and a Certificate of Appointment
to West Point, 2025—
the year he would have graduated.

We share the same birthday, he and I—
our fates intertwined yet never crossing,
except in the gentle March breeze

as I walk to school, listening
through half-open windows, to the soft
flap of curtains.

AFTERLIFE

On Tomb Sweeping Day
the one-hundred-and-sixth day
of the Chinese lunar calendar,
we sweep the tombstones of ancestors
and line them with chrysanthemums,
pay over two thousand *yuan*
for paper palaces, bicycles, laptops,
iPhones, chandeliers,
cruise ships, and Great Danes.

In Chinese, the word for filial piety
is *xiào shùn*, and our gifts to our ancestors
are dutiful offerings of protection,
like the ozone giving itself up
to absorb the rays of the sun,
or a new cornea shielding an ancient eye
from further wound, present sight
and aged wisdom seeking always
to embrace as one.

At the tombstones, we burn our joss sticks,
our ghost money, and papier-mâché
for the dead, fire's black shadows flicking
our feet, a serpent's tongue hissing of our
debts to the Afterlife—*there*,
in the flame's yellow tendrils, billowing
like coins spilling from the pockets
of *Shàngdì*, God of Heaven and all things.

VENUS IN RETROGRADE

in another life I am born / a knife-boned girl // speech
machines gutter / and scald our tongues // in another life
fire can't / be blue like his / hands, roaming and crackling
// in another life I swallow tar and / kiss him // the mouth
so domestic / caves in // a caramel pressed between lips
// I want to see him again / in summer / and jump over /
the narrowing necks of streams // in another life his heart
flattens / between my palms / and I teach him the way a
supernova can hurt // in another life spring never comes /
and he spills hunger / until it weeps out of me // in another
life I sift wine through his skin / until our muscles spasm /
into butterflies / and I make him faceless // in another life
I slot myself into him / like the weever makes its home /
beneath red sand

AUBADE AT POYANG LAKE

> *"Our motivation should not be fear, but hope."*
> — *Sir David Attenborough at the 2021 UN Climate Change*
> *Conference*

I am fifteen and I watch *Lǎo Lao*'s eyes glaze
over into rice paddies from her childhood

in China. One year, drought destroyed them,
brought a scarce and deadly yield of crops.

Living on their last bag of preserved
eggplant, her family scolded her for sneaking

vegetables to the livestock. They collected
rain for drinking water when lake beds

dried up, when sun burned through skin. I know
mouths can drink oil and bleed. Last year, I found

the cruel answer to Lǎo Lao's prayers: harvesting
paddies in Poyang Lake, the water was

too deep, we were too late—they had
drowned. I want a world where we don't

burn fossil fuels, rot ocean-lungs. One day,
my children should swim in clear waters, breathe

in fresh pine, play on the shore.

SELF-PORTRAIT WITH BREATH OF GHOSTS

Heavy rain and wind
whipped around
our dark house

as the night grew colder.
Our flashlights,
the steamy breath of ghosts

in the dead of winter.
My father's match
struck a stack

of miniature ebony logs
and turned them bright
orange, like the wings

of a monarch,
the dark body of the room
made thicker.

Over the flame, we boiled water
then cooled it
just long enough

to soak our feet—
calm ripples and soft circling
as the night wind raged.

The house stayed
black, but I memorized
how many steps

the stairway held,
the exact height of each step.

ALTAR FOR DAUGHTERHOOD

It's the night before your wedding.
In utero, I listen to anxiety crack

open your breastbone, persistent lightning as Pa
talks his mouth to rust. You always drank

papaya and banana smoothies
back then, yellow

sweetness puckering your skin like marmalade. Imagine
if I'd bitten our umbilical cord and held

your body's rotten song in my mouth
as it formed, as Pa loosened your tongue.

You would've baptized yourself, calculated
the distance you could've lassoed your hair

around Pa's neck. You would've torn out
my spine so he only had yours to worship.

Your breath tightens your legs, Ma.
From the nest, Ma, I can reach your thighs,

hold the wrinkled folds until they ebb. Can't you see
you are a summertime of brine turning

the seawall to sea, Ma? You were coating
your mouth in plum juice, waiting for God

to send a cardinal to scythe through
your stomach's pregnant sky. Until your eyes

hardened and itched, and girlhood—
as you knew it—was dead.

April 6th

I had a fever. I gave it
      to my parents. I didn't
think I would. I drank honeysuckle
      tea, slept as my cat

untangled my red headphones.
      I never thought
I'd miss it. The sound of
      clean tires over pebbles

engraved in the driveway. *Will I*
      hear it again?

    ✝

Ma says I am lucky
      to have a gurney. As we make our way
from the hospital parking lot,
      my head bumps.

Dr. Lam uncaps the swab
      with her teeth. *Breathe—*
Ma strokes my hair. She presses
      my head further back
onto the pillow.

I try not to stare. I have
      an unbridled urge
to heave. Instead I purse my lips.
      The moist tip of the swab dances
into my nose.

    ✝

Ma distracts me, whispers:
        In the name of humanity, before
deliquesce, salvage lives. I would
        question if it was a prayer
to the blessed healers, or all children
        of Mother Earth.

My aunts always told me
        Ma was never right in the head.

I am afraid to breathe.

        One-third in.
I stare cross-eyed at the stick, protruding—
        the doctor's hand does not shake.

Two-thirds in.
        I miss the way my breath cools
against my tongue as I purse my lips
        against the mouthpiece of my clarinet.
My most recent solo piece, *Abyss of Birds*, hums

        through my mind. The music pleads me
to perform the song
        for my dead cousins.

The swab prods my brain.
        Ma hunches over in the corner
of my eye.
        The vein in Dr. Lam's wrist protrudes.
My nose feels the warmth of her wrist.

BROTHER PORTRAIT, BLURRED

Dr. Longhi steps over the dead
        stored in rows, covers
his mouth with the mask
        he's been using for weeks.

My brothers' bodies shake,
        mouths agape like fish
gasping in the air
        they can't breathe.

My uncle falls to the ground,
        face angled toward the sky,
at the corner
        in front of the closed
furniture shop.

        Nobody dares approach him.
Supermarket cardboard
        stacked around the scene,
a wall—sacrifices
        must be made—

blue uniforms, a blur—
        the shriek of wheels,
the hospital bed rolling down
        the hall, the sharp inhale

of his breath, passing boys, passing
        girls, passing women and men
who shake like the last winter firs.

PREREQUISITE

You need to pack the bricks
of your house tight,

like an ensemble singing in unison,
to ensure no sound escapes.

When the storm ceases, you find
the wind erasing

the footsteps from your garden.
The wren's nest in the birdhouse

is untouched. The eggs would still hatch
if your cupped hands kept them warm.

The male wren perches on the fence,
another failed search for his mate.

Sometimes, what we need
is patience—

if, like the fox in the tapestry
on your wall, your eyes linger

too long on the prey,
the sly flick of the tail will give
you away before

you pounce. Meanwhile,
the frogs keep croaking,

the shadows keep racing
through the trees.

STEAM

On winter days
when my mom heats
water for tea,

I wait for the vapor
to become visible,
the steam so condensed

that I can pass
my hand through its ghost,
interrupting its slow

curling spirals
as I wonder about
the mysterious

fragility of air,
and why my dreams
are filled with the shape

of hot molecules,
their meanings a secret
even to myself,

and a desire for comfort
I cannot place.

MERCURY IN RETROGRADE

for Grandma (1937-2020)

Grandma lived on the river shore
all her life. Photos of her smile etched
in my mind as she puffs her chest out
clenching nets of fish. She found out
she was pregnant the day Grandpa took
that photo—a few months later,
a miscarriage: *High doses
of mercury*, the doctor said.

The mercury was undetectable
in the bodies of the fish, but they knew
the sky dosed the river
with it. There were

chickens also, few enough
to name. But soon,
the riverbeds dried—they had no choice
so Grandma and Grandpa began
eating the fish they had preserved. They collected
rain for drinking water, sheltered
like chickens inside once
the sun burnt their skin.

✝

Grandma told me this story
every time we ate the salmon we caught
at Amur River: *You know*, she starts as she cuts
the pink belly, *you don't know what's in 'em
till it hits you.* I always hugged her
from the back, wrapped my hands around
her stomach, careful of the caesarean scar. It was
a few shades darker than the salmon belly. Every night

beside me—for months—she'd thumb her lip
in prayer, say *It's all just children and love
and blood and bone.* She'd repeat it with precision
as if language itself could extract the mercury
from her blood, her tissue, her bone, her brain, her
memory—bit by poisonous bit.

NIGHT WATCH

A racoon circles
a shadowy grave
as I watch
from my bedroom window
on 34th Street.
Her eyes are
golden rims
like my own
through these weeks
of sleeplessness
since my canary died,
and the days became
marked
by the absence of her song,
which my violin cannot replace,
even as my fingers try
to match the melody
of her voice.
Each time I try
to fill this silence,
I only find more shadow,
alone in my room.

The racoon is like a Valkyrie,
a maiden goddess
in ancient Norse mythology
known to sift through
the souls of those slain in battle,
carefully assigning
worthy heroes
to the afterlife,
and the yellow
of the raccoon's eyes
reminds me of yellow wings,
and of the word
canary—

as light as my resined
bow playing
into the cool grey
of the early morning.

LAST BUTTERSCOTCH

Ma's tiger rug catches dust
as our copy of *The Cask of Amontillado*
sits, untouched, on the shelf.

Layers of snow paw
my bedroom window—
my persistent desire
for Ma's touch eclipsed by knowing
she won't give it again.

Each night, Ma pounds
dried berries into powder,
sprinkles them into
a bowl of hot water.

Listening to the march
of the pestle, my tongue swirls
the last butterscotch
she gave me—
I can taste the milk
rotten with age.

Then, as she soaks her feet,
and thinks of all the ways
her daughter once laughed,
the house turns silent—
my toes, winter-bitten, curl slowly
under my blanket.

Under pink moons, the snow
gleams through the icicles. My hands—
peach-skinned, chapped
by winter, itch and itch for her touch.

ELEGY WITH LIPSTICK SMEAR

for my friend Delilah (2002-2018)

I.

She couldn't be more of a virgin
if she tried, one girl said by the lockers.

Delilah's throat, glassed. Her voice, gunked.
Saying to the girls: *I am not a prude.*

Sweet naiveté, her father whispered in her ear
the night before. Her throat, itching

like beach-flea bites. Later that night,
her mother cradled Delilah's head

in her arms. Then, Delilah asked—

                    Do you love me or Father more?

She was silent. Hours passed, ataraxic, in sleep.

✝

Her father enters her bedroom, no knock. He tears
the blanket off her body, then pulls

her blinds open. She is used
to this. He hands her a prescription bottle. Two white

tablets under her tongue, no water. She chews
and chews, the bitter white hiding

behind her teeth, until they are thin

as trust. Her head is lighter ... it is
leaking water—she lifts her hand,

as her mother walks in with a glass, to refuse it.

✝

Snip. Delilah grips the scissors, cutting the outline
of Mother's sun-smoked face. The family

collage won't make itself, so she presses
against Father's cheek on the tapestry

above her headboard. The corner of her lips
twitch. She resists turning

the scissors 180 degrees. She is careful
not to harm her father. Her nails scratch

her mother's cut-out face, the deep red
lipstick smearing down her chin.

                    II.

One night, Mother serves me
ten slices of pineapple and a glass
of cranberry juice. She watches me drink.

As I drink, Father tucks a strand of hair
behind my ear. I smell
his breath, spoiled
milk, as he whispers—

                              "Did you eat them?"

I hesitate. His fingers paw

my cheeks, waiting for my blush

to ripen to *Coquette's Serenade*,
the shade of Mother's lipstick
when they were wed.

That night, Mother told me
I was too sour: "Giving
your body is something
you'll get used
to." All night, I prayed
for a pineapple
with a razor core.

AFTERGLOW

There I was, bathing in goat milk
and rose petals again. Again, Mother

washing away the blood
from my breasts, inner thighs.
Her lips were thin.

Every time she washed, she was
rougher and rougher, until I wanted

to loop her blonde locks
around my finger and tug.

✝

Once, when I wasn't on my medication,
I begged her to stop—
Please.

She opened her mouth like a fish. *You did this
to yourself*. Her lips shut.

That night, I pulled out
the silkiest locks from the crown
of her head.

✝

The next day, at school, I was proud
of my face's afterglow. The way

my emerald eyes became more
yellow each day, yellow
to match my skin.

Wasn't I beautiful?

✝

For months, I wished to see my brother again.
I thought of his last day here, walking in

as my father checked
my back molars with a finger.

✝

That day, the humidifier broke.
As I ate, my nose bled across
the yellow flesh
of leftover pineapple.

We lived on the sixth floor. I watched
the street below as I bled, wondering
when he would return.

✝

When I was done, I sliced
a row of clementines in half, realized

like fruit, every tongue had
a different texture.

Father had a sandpaper tongue.

✝

Stars littered the sky until I slept.

I slipped off my shirt, sat
on the edge of my bed.

✝

That night, Mother tucked
the blanket up to my neck.

Her hands slid to the corners.

The crease on my throat faded
when we heard two knocks.

WHITE PEN

A dove's white wings
depend on the blackest
night skies to seem
whiter, the same way
failure teaches a child after
she falls and is bruised
to watch out for the stones
hidden in shadows,
or how a dancer attempts
a grand jeté and stumbles,
decides she must try again
for the perfect landing,
even if she never reaches it—
learning that the pursuit
will always be more delicious
than the outcome—which is
not so different from a mother
raising her child to believe
in perfection, but learning
that imperfection is more beautiful,
wrinkles on a forehead,
the beaten pages
of a beloved paperback,
or the rushed script
of an artist chasing her idea—

MARIE

*for Marie Colvin, who dedicated her life
to the freedom of the press (1956-2012)*

She wore pink socks in the documentary.
An eye lost to war, coated in dust, Marie
flailing like a baby lapping for breastmilk.
She interviewed a woman: mother of two
infants, one crushed beneath a building,
another waiting for a father who keeps
vanishing through stone archways.
Doctors bang their heads against walls
and all the mothers have forgotten white streams.
Another heart held in pumping hands, another
family of mouths itching for prayer, no monitor
to announce it's stopped. Bone on bone, bone
in wine, bones that decay. She used her gym card
to trick the border officers into thinking
she was a nurse. Now stories are warping across
the faces of graves. Nightingales emerge
but their screams are printed in the newspaper.
Mass graves make women into widows
of war, willow-bodied, bowing clothed heads, as if two
clasped hands will stitch together, will meld
crushed bone, then explode—as bodies wash up
on Oyster Bay shores, filled with the sand
of every childhood memory I keep: tasting
the sand, building castles with it, burying myself
in it, waiting for the tide to rise.

KILL LIST

The teachers didn't tell us
until weeks later.

They ushered us
in closets and behind drawers.

Under teachers' desks
and behind vending machines.

The speaker blared,
evident shaking

in our principal's voice,
ordering teachers to group students.

Some flicked their wrists,
flippant sighs

like bay leaves
gently tapping the ground.

My friend prayed, found
comfort in the crook of my neck.

Flashback: stubbed crayons,
a lost ruler,

wads of purple gum
stuck to chair legs, dried to clay.

We still wait with bitter breath.

THE BLUE ROSE

They say a blue rose
is impossible
to grow without cloning
the gene for delphinidin
from petunias—
but even then,
the pigment is more
mauve or lilac, not
the color of that moment
when evening begins
to bleed into day, not
the color of the deep end
of a swimming pool,
or the berries
from my grandma's greenhouse,
or the floral swirls on the teacups
from Shenzhen, or the silk
of French kings, or lapis lazuli
in Renaissance painting,
or the sculptures of Yves Klein
I've only read about,
never seen up close,
and not like the blue of
the crystal I found
in the corner of a cave when
my family hiked
through the mountains
of Emei
and stopped to share
a vinegar salad,
bottles of fruit water,
an extra canteen of ice.

CATALOGUE OF RIPENING

Turning supple skin to wrinkles,
the green lychee pricks to spikes.

✝

When the plums are hard,
leave them in the garage

until they are as soft
as a robin's underbelly.

✝

Sift the dirt from Mother's
white petunias through
your esophagus

to grow a girl. Hide
the pebbles and stones
under your tongue

until the green of your veins
fades to grey.

✝

Light the jasmine candle
and drip wax down

your arms until the peach
turns pink.

✝

Your house shelters
no infant, so cradle yourself.

✝

Make sure to steady
your head with your right palm

and listen to the birdsong—
the rhythm catches you by surprise
and you awaken.

ACKNOWLEDGMENTS

I wish to thank the editors of the following publications, judges of various contests, and organizations that have published or recognized poems in this chapbook, some in earlier versions:

Best Teen Writing: "Sacrifice"; reprinted in *Polyphony Lit*

COUNTERCLOCK: "Brother Portrait, Blurred"

FERAL: A Journal of Poetry and Art: "Venus in Retrograde"

The Hippocrates Prize Anthology: "Pink Milk"

Movable Type: "Elegy with Lipstick Smear"

Nuclear Age Peace Foundation: "Open Sun"

The Poetry Society of the UK: "65 Cybele," "Kill List"

The Poetry Society of Virginia: "Afterlife"

Raleigh Review: "Afterglow"

Stone Soup: "The Money Tree," "Steam," and "Self-Portrait: Breath of Ghosts"

West Trestle Review: "Catalogue of Ripening," "Kyoto"

Young Poets Network: "Aubade at Poyang Lake"

1455: "坏事好事 Huài Shì Hǎo Shì (Evil Things, Good Things)"; reprinted by Penn State Behrend and *Stone Soup*

Thank you to the Alliance for Young Artists & Writers, Young Poets Network, Poetry Society of the UK, Academy of American Poets, *Adroit Journal*, and *Stone Soup* for bestowing tremendous opportunities for writing and growth.

ABOUT THE AUTHOR

Sabrina Guo is a young writer and activist from New York. The youngest global winner of the Poems to Solve the Climate Crisis challenge, she spoke out against climate injustice and performed her winning poem in the 2021 UN Climate Change Conference (COP26). She has received the Civic Expression Award, the Foyle Young Poets of the Year Award, nine national medals from the Scholastic Art & Writing Awards, and was recognized by the Adroit Prizes and the Bennington College Young Writers Awards. Her work has been published in *Best Teen Writing, Raleigh Review, West Trestle Review,* and *Counterclock,* among others. The founder of Girl Pride International and Long Island Laboring Against COVID-19, Sabrina's writing and humanitarian work have been profiled by Disney and Long Island Business News 30 Under 30, and were recognized by President George H.W. Bush's Daily Point of Light Award, the Princeton Prize in Race Relations, and the President's Lifetime Achievement Award.

CPSIA information can be obtained
at www.ICGtesting.com
Printed in the USA
LVHW100535181122
733278LV00039B/2422